"I might not have gone where I intended to go, but I ended up where I needed to be" - Douglas Adams

This book is for the ones who have loved deeply, lost painfully, and found themselves somewhere in between.

For the ones still healing, still growing, still learning that they were never broken; just unfolding.

These poems are a mirror, a map, and a conversation between past and present. I hope you find yourself somewhere in these words.

Thank you for choosing to read my little book.

♡ With all my Love

Mimi x

For Those I Hold in My Heart

For Lilly, Arthur, and Herbie;
the best things I've ever done:
You are my rhythm, my reason;
the chapters I'd write again and again.
For my dear dad, who still walks beside
me in the quiet,
Whose guidance is woven into every
word I'll ever write.
For the friends who left too soon;
you are not gone, but dearly missed:
You still live in the stories, and the
kindness that sings, long after my room
falls quiet.
And for the ones who stand by me still;
who know the mess and the magic;
you have held me up, poured the tea
and reminded me who I am,
and indeed who I am not;
these words, they belong to you too.

M x

TRUEST BEAUTY

And perhaps...

It wasn't her face,

or the accolades she gathered;

but her unbreakable spirit,

her boldness to believe in light,

even when shadows crept close.

A fierce brightness lived within her,

running wild and free,

igniting everything she touched,

and that,

in the end,

was her truest beauty.

WHAT ARE YOU WILLING TO LET GO OF?

A cat that dreams of becoming a lion must lose its taste for rats:
You cannot feast on scraps and expect to rule the savannah.

Greatness is not about grasping;? It's about releasing. You cannot rise while clinging to the weight of old ways. Comfort will cradle you, whisper that you are safe, but it is a cage dressed as a sanctuary.

Procrastination will soothe you with promises of tomorrow. Excuses will pile up, stacking themselves like bricks between you and the life you were meant to live.

Let go.

Of what no longer serves you.
Of what keeps you small.
Of the fear that convinces you to wait.

Replace hesitation with discipline.
Replace distraction with purpose.
Trade doubt for a belief that refuses to break.

Ask yourself; what are you still holding on to?

And more importantly; what could you become if you finally let go?

STEP OFF THE STAGE

Half your life is spent in borrowed smiles,
in careful words; in measured miles.
Half of life is spent on stage,
learning lines, suppressing rage.

We twist, we bend, we shine, we fade;
caught in the dance of roles we've played.
We seek their nods, their soft applause,
chained to their rules; bound by their laws.

And when the curtain starts to close,
we count the cost of what we chose;
the restless nights, the silent wars,
the love withheld, the closing doors.

But listen now; the echoes call,
"Enough, enough, let the curtain fall."
No more the mask, no more the reins,
no more the weight of others' names.

Step from the play, leave the stage,
write your story on a different page.
For life is not a role to rehearse,
but a soul untamed, a universe.

ONE MORE DAY WITH YOU

If I could have one more day with you it isn't the
grand gestures I'd seek, nor extraordinary days;
but rather the quiet, ordinary moments: a walk
with the dog, soup shared on conversations about
the garden, pretending nothing had changed,
when in fact, everything had.

I'd fill every silence with the questions I
never thought to ask, and hold every
word you spoke like the rarest of
treasures, knowing how swiftly they'd
fade.

I'd tell you, softly yet fiercely, how
incomplete I've felt without you, how
deep the ache when I remember your
absence.

Before our time ran out once more,
I'd wrap my arms around you the
way we cling to things we cannot
bear to lose.

You would remind me gently, that life
is not meant to be lived in the shadows
of yesterday, that your presence is
threaded through every fibre of who I
am, encouraging me to step forward
without always needing to understand.

And as I struggled to stay brave, you
would tell me this isn't our last goodbye;
that the moment I stop searching for you
will be the moment I've found my way to
you again.

Because when that day comes,
you are the first I'll look for, you,
who taught me how to live, even
after you're out of sight.

BE ALL IN...

Perhaps;

it's far better to dance barefoot,

thighs jiggling, laughter wild,

than to wake one day

with nothing but regret in your pocket.

Write the messy book,

paint with fearless hands,

chase the fire that sets your soul ablaze;

no half-measures.

Perfection is a thief,

stealing moments too precious to lose.

So dive in, heart-first,

no tiptoeing in the shallows.

If you're going to do it; be all in.

Live boldly. Love joyfully.

Let your days be full, your spirit untamed.

For the deepest heartbreak

is not what you did;

but what you never dared to do.

Or risk meeting your own reflection years from now,

eyes filled with the ache of a life half-lived.

WHO YOU WERE...

Who you were kept you safe;
taught you caution, built your walls,
held your heart in careful hands
so it wouldn't break.

But who you are becoming?
That is who will set you free.

Step beyond the edges of comfort,
breathe in the wide brave unknown.
There is a life waiting;
where fear loosens its grip
and wings replace chains.

**You were never meant
to stay the same.**

AND SO...

It isn't the size of your home,
the exams you've passed,
the position at work,
or even the length of your marriage;
but the quality of your relationships,
the connections that shape the very fabric of your life.

Friends, bosses, the wandering souls and even the playful kitty cats,
fathers, and partners; these are the bonds that matter most. Invest in
them, for within lies a wealth beyond measure; a treasure trove of
warmth, memories, support, and guidance.

So when your mind flashes back to moments;
when laughter sent tears rolling down your cheeks,
or a shared secret left you both on the verge of tears;
let that be your cue: your heart is whispering,
"Reconnect, recharge what makes life truly beautiful."

So here's a gentle nudge before today slips into tomorrow:
pick up the phone, send that text.
Remember, the happiest memories are seldom made alone.
Whether friend, lover, or cherished kin,
together, with a little effort,
we gather the sweet, nourishing ingredients
for a life rich and juicy it will truly fulfil.

ONE OF MY FAVOURITE PARTS

You didn't stay until the final chapter,
but your words still echo between the pages
I reach for you in empty lines,
where your laughter used to live.

The story continued without you,
but I cannot change the chapters,
without tracing the crease where you left.

The corner is folded down,
not to revisit pain,
but to honour the beauty
of the moments we shared together,

You were one of my favorite parts,
even if you weren't there for the ending.

And *maybe*, that's enough.

WOULD YOU LIKE A CUPPA

I asked if you'd like tea, but what I
meant was: **I see you**.

I want to hold space for you,
to offer warmth; a quiet moment where the
world softens.

I asked if you had eaten, but what I meant was: **You
are precious to me**.

I want to fill you up;
not just with food, but with comfort,
with care, with all the wonders life has to
offer.

I asked how your day was, but what I wished was for all
your days to be kind. That worry would never weigh on
your shoulders, that I could gather your burdens in my
hands and make them lighter

I said your hair looked great, but what I meant was:
You are beautiful to me.

Not because of strands and curls, but
because of the way you laugh, the way you
move through the world, the way you are
wholly, completely you.

Love is not always loud,
not always grand. Sometimes,
it's a cup of tea,

a warm meal, a simple question, a
quiet knowing; the smallest things,
carrying the deepest meaning.

SUCCESS...

Success isn't measured by someone else's ruler.
It isn't found in comparison, or ticking off boxes,
or in chasing a life that you didn't choose for yourself.

It lives in the warm joy of being at ease with yourself,
in the magic of doing things your way, in the small,
steady moments that make you feel you're who you want to be,

It's not shaped by your parents' hopes,
your friends' expectations,
or the endless scroll of what should be.
It's yours to write; every day, in every choice you make.

So, listen closely.
Follow what lights you up.
Build a life that feels like home.

You hold the pen.
You set the pace.
Define success in a way that's true to you;
then go after it, fully and fearlessly.

TRAUMA..

It's not what happened to you.
It's not the war,
not the abuse,
not the pain you endured.

It is the wound left behind;
the unseen scar beneath the surface,
the echo that lingers long after the moments have passed.

It is not the event itself,
but the footprint left behind,
the way it shapes you differently as you walk the world,
the way it teaches you to brace for a storm
even when the skies are clear.

AND PERHAPS...

It's not the why that truly matters;
the reasons they left, the words
they chose, the promises they
broke with quiet disregard.

For the why is a maze without exit, an
endless puzzle without prize, a search
that leaves you empty, wandering
through shadows of doubt, always
hungry for an answer you may never
find.

Instead, ask yourself the what: What has
this taught your kindly heart? What story
do you now tell yourself, and does it lift
you, or weigh you down? What meaning
do you weave from threads left tangled,
from silences left unfilled?

Your feelings need no validation;
they are yours, they are real, and
their worth does not rely on
understanding another's actions.

Fixating on their why is dancing on the edge of
someone else's storm, hoping not to get caught
in the rain. But your power lies elsewhere: in
choosing where you step next, in rewriting your
narrative, in gathering lessons like quiet
treasures from the rubble.

So let the unanswered why fade softly;
like echoes disappearing into night. The
what is where your strength begins; it's
where healing grows wings and gently,
bravely, you will take flight again.

Be careful where you drink for some would slip you poison,

just to watch you fall.

Drink only from the well of grace,
Show all about integrity, kindness and stand strong and tall.

MAYBE...

It isn't in being understood
that peace is truly found, but in quietly
releasing the need to convince those who
choose not to see.

Because people can only meet you,
as deeply as they've met themselves.

And so, the real freedom
comes in letting go;
in accepting that being misunderstood,
even disliked,
will not dim your light,
not silence your truth.

In surrendering this struggle,
you'll find calm waiting softly;
a quiet courage raising,
allowing you, at last,
to live exactly as you are.

TO WOMEN

We are the lifeline;
bringing life into an unkind world,
bravely sowing seeds of hope
where greed once thrived,
turning hate into words that heal.

We are mothers and sisters,
friends, aunts, lovers;
arms open wide
for those whose life has grown too heavy,
still standing tall;
even when the world arrives late
to recognise our worth.

I pray we do better:
more respect, more safety,
more breaths spent
speaking of our value and sharing love,
for tomorrow is never promised.
Let us rise for all women;
for every daughter;
bearing the torch passed down
by those who came before,
and lighting the path
for those yet to come.

Dear Friend,

I won't ask what they did.
I can see it in your smile;
how it falters at the edges
like a page worn thin from re-reading
the same sour ending.

I won't ask,
because some stories deserve silence
more than they deserve air.

But I will say this:

Forgive them.
Not loudly.
Not with trumpets or grace.
Not in a way that suggests they matter more
than your mornings do.

Forgive them
quietly, stubbornly,
like planting wildflowers
where they once scorched the earth.

Because this;
this life;
is short, and astonishing,
and can feel really hard,
without dragging their ghosts
over your every sunrise.

Forgiveness is not a welcome mat.
It's not tea and sympathy for the unrepentant.
It is not martyrdom in a prettier dress.

It is choosing not to drink poison
just because they poured it.

It is an elegant rebellion.
The kind that says,
"I will not build my future
on the architecture of your damage."

You don't owe them healing.
But you do owe yourself the right
to live untethered from the gravity of their ruin.

Let go.
Let it fall from your hands
like a letter you never need to send.

Let it go
not because they asked,
not because they'll change,
but because your soul deserves
to stretch its limbs again.

Forgiveness is not for them.
It's for the you
you haven't met yet;
the one who wakes up without the ache,
who laughs before stepping into the room,
who stops rewriting the past
as if it might finally turn kind.

So write this instead:

"I survived you.
And that is the last thing you get."

Then fold that truth
into your pocket,
and walk forward;
lighter, fiercer,
unapologetically free.

With tenderness, and teeth,
From Me x

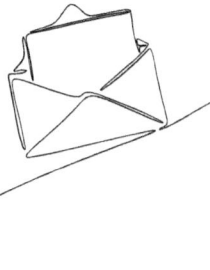

ROSE TINTED GLASSES

And perhaps,
when you wear those rose-tinted glasses,
all the warnings blur softly,
fading gently into scenery,
flags ruffling in the colourful breeze.

But clarity comes quietly,
in the space after goodbye;
where truth whispers softly
that flags waved red all along,
and your heart simply chose to hope.

See clearly now, trust the colours life
shows you. The truth was always
there; it only asked you;
remove your rose coloured shades.

REBUILD WITH WORDS

Speak words that mend the cracks;
like gentle mortar for a wounded heart.
Where hurt once lived, let
kindness and hope settle in:

Because a soft phrase,
shared at the right moment,
can rebuild the places
others thought forever lost.

The Sacred Trinity (of Friendship)

You don't need fifty friends or a buzzing WhatsApp group;
"Hot Girls Summer" might be fun (though it hasn't been hot since '02),
but all you really need is just three.

One: The Truth Teller
She isn't here to sugarcoat your life.
Sipping her oat milk flat white, she calls out your nonsense:
"You think he might change?"
She says, "He won't. Block him."
No fluff; just the hard, cold facts.
She's like your soul's personal trainer,
minus the protein powder and over the top positivity.

Two: The Confidant
Keeper of your deepest secrets and sacred messes,
the therapist you don't pay (but really should).
When you text, "I did something silly,"
she replies, "Tell me everything;
The kettle is on."
Zero judgment, maximum snacks.
She holds your shame like fine china;
never dropping a single piece.

Three: The Ride or Die

This friend's got bail money and a shovel on speed dial.
No lengthy explanations needed; just say, "Come now."
In six minutes flat, she'll be there; hoodie on, snacks packed,
engine running.
The kind of friend who's got your back
even when you forget your own spine.

And if, by some cosmic miracle, you find all three in one
glittering, chaos-taming human?

Frame her, feed her, and never let her go.
Because friendship isn't measured by matching tattoos, or
perfectly curated holiday reels.

It's about who shows up when your mascara's running,
when your ex is texting, when your brain's whirling at 3 a.m.

No, you don't need a crowd; you need the right crew.

Just three.

The right three.

LOVE IS NEVER THE ISSUE

You didn't walk away because your love ran out; You left because you were exhausted from holding everything together alone, love can only stretch so far when it's one person carrying all the weight, doing all the work, making all the effort, while the other simply assumes they'll always remain.

You can love someone deeply and still feel utterly alone beside them,
You can adore them and still feel invisible,
unheard, unvalued, drained; The future unfathomable Love doesn't heal neglect, fix broken promises, or erase the times you felt guilty for needing to feel a fragment of effort returned.

Relationships don't end because love deminishes.
They end because effort fades,
because one stops choosing the other,
because one person ceases to take the steps forward needed,
comfort might quietly slip into indifference.

If you want love to thrive, don't just say it;
show it.
Consistently.
Be present,
be attentive,
Take the steps, even when it's hard,
make them certain of their worth.

Because love, without genuine effort,
is just a beautiful excuse.

'But, I love you.'

DON'T FORGET THEM

When You Had Nothing to Say
And in that quiet place,
there were those who listened anyway;
who stayed when you tried to push them away,
who gave without expecting a thing,
who believed you deserved more,
even when you didn't believe it yourself.

They forgave you
when you couldn't forgive yourself,
celebrated your smallest victories,
found you in your darkest corners,
and loved you
when you felt unlovable.

They apologised
not because they had to,
but because they cared.
And they showed it, and showed up
not just with their words.

Don't forget them.

My Dear,

if you dream of being spectacular:
of lighting up the dark,
of writing your name in stars:
you must first make peace
with being misunderstood.

The desire to be spectacular and accepted
is a core human paradox.
We ache to be seen,
but we also long to belong.
And sometimes, the price of belonging
is the soft betrayal of your own brilliance.

But remember this:
to have an uncommon life,
you must become an uncommon person.

The crowd does not clap
for those who leave the script.
They will call you odd,
too much, too bold:
until one day they call you brilliant.

You cannot walk the average path
and expect an extraordinary view.
You cannot shrink to fit
and still expect to soar.

Normal shoes were never made
for wild feet like yours.

So go.
Be too much.
Be wildly yourself.
Be the strange and shining thing
you were born to be.

And when you feel lonely on the path,
remember:
the view is always clearest
from the places few are brave enough to go.

IT'S TRUE...

You can't begin the next chapter
if you keep re-reading the last one.

The past, inked in familiar lines,
may comfort you with its worn pages,
but real growth lies in the blank spaces;
the unwritten story still waiting to unfold.

Let go of old words,
allow them to fade into the background,
so you can step forward,
ready to embrace the promise of a tomorrow
holding all you've ever hoped for.

OH, GENTLE ONE

You are the kind of soul
who cries at Bridget Jones,
and slows to rescue a wounded bird or bunny;
who notices the subtle shift in a neighbours smile;
please, don't change.

We have so very many blinkered folk,
Unable to see beyond the peripheral of their own destination.

Your gentle, luminous being
guides us home to what really matters.

So please keep feeling and noticing,
keep being exactly who you are.
Because in a world that barely scratches the surface;
it is your tender bravery
that will remind us;
empathy is the fiercest trait of them all.

And perhaps...

It doesn't need to be perfect
to be amazing, beautiful,
and to reshape your life
in the most unexpected,
wonderful ways. Sometimes, it's the
imperfect edges that catch the light
and make everything shine.

♡

If Integrity Was...

If integrity was a voice,
she would never shout, nor waver;
she would speak in steady tones,
like the tide greeting the shore,
like the moon pulling the sea,
unchanged by the noise of the world.

If integrity was a road,
she would be quiet, unbeaten,
etched with the footsteps of those
who chose truth over ease,
who walked not to be seen,
but to be certain of their own path.

If integrity was a fire,
she would not rage for attention,
but burn with quiet conviction,
forging steel in the distance,
melting away the need for approval.

If integrity was a weight,
it would nestle deep in your bones,
not heavy, but immovable,
holding you upright
when the world tries to bend you.

If integrity was a currency,
she would neither inflate with flattery,
nor diminish in darkness;
she would be the rarest of treasures,
worth more under pressure,
untouched by shifting tides.

And if integrity was a choice,
it would not be made once,
but over and over again,
not for applause,
not for proof,
but because some things
are simply who you are.

BLOOM

It's time to bloom, my friend,
for it has always been your time.

Paint the world in all your hues,
no need to stay so small. Of all
the gardens in all the land, you
are the brightest of them all.

Unfurl your petals,
stand tall,
lift your face to the sun
and take your place among the wild and the magnificent,

The time is now, my love;
to open, to rise,
to give this world
everything that was always meant to be yours.

So bloom, my love, bloom.

A DIFFERENT ENDING

We do not love as blank slates.
We love with the hands we were taught to hold with,
the words we learned to speak through closed doors,
the silence we mistook for safety.

We love with the echoes of childhood;
with bruises that look like boundaries,
with longing shaped like loyalty,
with hearts taught to chase what runs.

And still, we ask ourselves,
why this person?
Why this impossible love,
this push and pull that exhausts
and yet, somehow, completes us?

Why not the soft one,
the calm one,
the one who answers every message
and never raises their voice?

Because somewhere deep down,
we are not seeking perfection.
We are seeking familiarity.
We are seeking a second chance
at a moment we were too small to understand;
where love walked away,
or looked through us,
or only showed up when we hurt.

And so we fall for the ones
who carry the storm
that first taught us what love might feel like.
We stay not for the chaos;
but for the hope
that this time,
someone might stay.

That this time,
we won't have to raise our voice
to be heard.
That this time,
we might undo the ending,
rewrite the chapter
where love left,
and stayed gone.

To grow in love
with someone who meets you
at the aching places
without fear;
this is the rarest thing.

But if you find it,
if you both stay long enough
to learn a new language,
to quiet the ghosts,
to soften the reflex to run;

Then you are not just loving.
You are healing.
You are rewriting history
with hands no longer trembling.

You are choosing
a different ending.

AND PERHAPS...

She spent too many years staring at her old life,
wondering why the days felt so heavy,
why her soul wore its weariness like a second skin.

But one day, as if a gentle knock tapping at
the door of her heart, a new thought arrived:
start a new chapter, write a new story.

Easier said than done, yet she woke each morning
changing one small thing; a breath, a choice, a tiny
thought; and bit by bit;
the grey edges of her world began to brighten.

*She certainly won't tell you
she got it right every time:*

But still, she kept going, kept battling, kept
believing. And soon, little sparks of hope grew
into steady flames, lighting the path forward.

Now, she stands on the other side of
happiness; not all at once, but one day at a
time. Excuse her, please, while she steps back
into the sunlight, ready to evolve, ready to live.

Happiness & You—The Perfect Two

Happiness;
she is not a finish line to be crossed,
nor a prize at the end of the race.
She does not wait in the next chapter,
the next lover,
or the next, shinier version of you.
She is here.
In the sunlight spilling through the trees,
the melody of a song you had forgotten,
the warmth of a hand that does not let go.
She lingers in the smallest of things;
the way morning light spills across your pillow,
the quiet joy of bare feet on dewy grass,
the laughter lines in a familiar face.
Happiness is not something you win,
but something you welcome.
Not a destination,
but a way of walking.
Hold her lightly; without fear,
and watch how she grows.
For even when she drifts away,
as all things do,
open your eyes;
and you'll see she was never far.
Because happiness was never something to own;
only something to share,
to give away freely,
knowing that in doing so,
she will always return.
And you...
you were never meant to walk this life alone.

Happiness and you;
the perfect two.

Beautiful Concoction

And maybe; she isn't merely strong,
fierce, or honest;
but a wondrous blend of it all,
a quiet storm: gentle yet unyielding,
softness dancing with strength,
truth spoken without apology.

She's the woman whose side you choose
when the world is at war,
for within her quiet bravery lies a force;
a magnetic strength that draws you in,
making you stronger just by being near.

She isn't one to oppose;
she's your collaborator,
an ally whose spirit braves the way
even through the fiercest storms.

To every woman whose complexity,
grace, and inner fire ensures she voice is
heard.

GOOD BYE FOR NOW

Thank you for sharing these pages with me, it really means a lot. If my words have found a home in your heart, know that I wrote them with you in mind. This book is just a collection of moments; some mine, some yours, some we may share without ever meeting.

I hope you walk away feeling a little more seen.

Mimi x

If this book spoke to you, I'd love to hear from you;
You can connect with me at @mimi.g.musings.

www.ingramcontent.com/pod-product-compliance
Lightning Source LLC
Chambersburg PA
CBHW020446030426
42337CB00014B/1425